ZIMBABWE

By Donna Reynolds
and Alicia Z. Klepeis

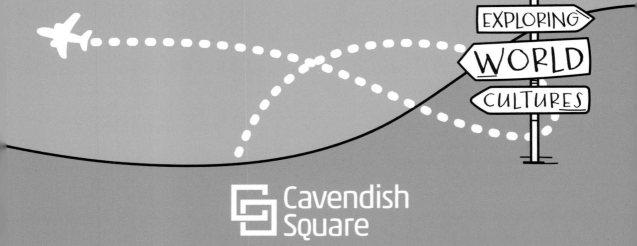

EXPLORING WORLD CULTURES

Cavendish Square

Published in 2024 by Cavendish Square Publishing, LLC
2544 Clinton Street, Buffalo, NY 14224

Library of Congress Cataloging-in-Publication Data

Names: Reynolds, Donna, 1976- author. | Klepeis, Alicia, 1971- author.
Title: Zimbabwe / by Donna Reynolds and Alicia Z. Klepeis.
Other titles: Exploring world cultures.
Description: Second edition | Buffalo, NY : Cavendish Square Publishing,
   [2024] | Series: Exploring world cultures | Includes bibliographical
   references and index.
Identifiers: LCCN 2023035642 | ISBN 9781502669995 (library binding) | ISBN
   9781502669988 (paperback) | ISBN 9781502670007 (ebook)
Subjects: LCSH: Zimbabwe--Juvenile literature.
Classification: LCC DT2889 .K54 2024 | DDC 968.91--dc23/eng/20230801
LC record available at https://lccn.loc.gov/2023035642

Writers: Alicia Z. Klepeis; Donna Reynolds (second edition)
Editor: Jennifer Lombardo
Copyeditor: Danielle Haynes
Designer: Andrea Davison-Bartolotta

Find us on

CONTENTS

Introduction 4

Chapter 1   Geography 6

Chapter 2   History 8

Chapter 3   Government .10

Chapter 4   The Economy 12

Chapter 5   The Environment 14

Chapter 6   The People Today 16

Chapter 7   Lifestyle 18

Chapter 8   Religion 20

Chapter 9   Language 22

Chapter 10   Arts and Festivals 24

Chapter 11   Fun and Play 26

Chapter 12   Food 28

Glossary 30

Find Out More 31

Index 32

INTRODUCTION

The African country of Zimbabwe has gone through many changes in its history. People have lived in the area for thousands of years. Different groups ruled what is now Zimbabwe during its history. Zimbabwe is an independent country today.

In the countryside, many people in Zimbabwe grow food and raise animals. In the cities, they have the same kinds of jobs as people in other cities around the world. No matter where they live, Zimbabweans enjoy music, art, books, and sports.

Zimbabwe has set aside some parts of the country, such as Lake Kariba (shown here), as wildlife reserves.

There are many beautiful places to visit in Zimbabwe. The country has waterfalls, mountains, grasslands, and valleys. Tourists, or visitors, come from all over the world to see Zimbabwe's wildlife and historical places.

Like many other countries, Zimbabwe has some problems. The government doesn't always treat its people well. Also, many Zimbabweans have trouble finding and paying for food. Zimbabweans love their country and want it to be the best it can be, so many are working to fix these problems.

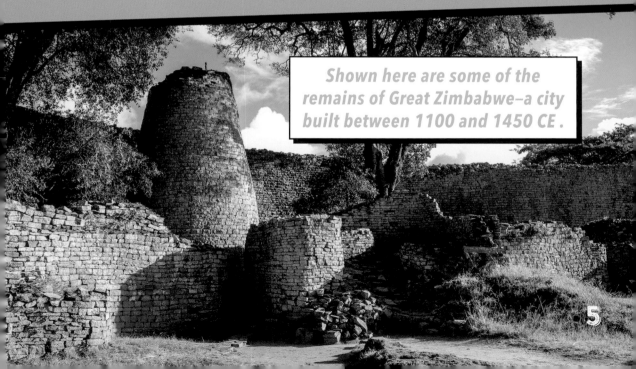

Shown here are some of the remains of Great Zimbabwe–a city built between 1100 and 1450 CE .

Zimbabwe covers about 150,872 square miles (390,757 square kilometers). It's a little bigger than the U.S. state of Montana. The countries of Botswana, Mozambique, South Africa, and Zambia border Zimbabwe. It's landlocked, which means it doesn't border any oceans. However, it does have several rivers. These include the Zambezi, Limpopo, Runde, and Save Rivers.

Victoria Falls is on the border of Zambia and Zimbabwe.

FACT!

June is generally Zimbabwe's coolest month, and October is generally its warmest month.

Most of Zimbabwe is a high **plateau**. An area called the Highveld, which is about 5,000 feet (1,520 meters) high, covers about 25 percent of the country. It runs from the country's southwest to its northeast. This area is great for farming.

THE MIDDLEVELD

The second-highest part of Zimbabwe, which is called the Middleveld, is between 3,000 and 4,000 feet (914 and 1,219 m) high. It covers about 40 percent of the country.

HISTORY

The San people are related to the first people who lived in what is now Zimbabwe around 500,000 years ago. Between the 5th and 10th centuries, Bantu peoples arrived. They made the San move into the desert and took over their land. Another group, the Shona, started building a city called Great Zimbabwe around 1100 CE. Great Zimbabwe was an important center for trading and religion, or faith.

The bird on Zimbabwe's flag is based on this carving, or small figure, found at Great Zimbabwe.

The Portuguese, Dutch, and British controlled countries around Zimbabwe in the 1800s. They wanted to move into Zimbabwe for **economic** reasons. These included enslaving Zimbabweans, looking for gold, and building a railroad to move goods and people around Africa. It wasn't until 1980 that Zimbabwe became an independent country with the name it has today.

Robert Mugabe was Zimbabwe's leader from 1980 to 2017.

THE UDI

In 1965, Rhodesia announced the Unilateral Declaration of Independence (UDI). This meant the country told Great Britain it would no longer have control. However, it took 15 more years for Rhodesia to become the country of Zimbabwe.

Zimbabwe's full name is the **Republic** of Zimbabwe. Its government has three parts, or branches. The legislative part of the government is known as Parliament. People in Parliament write new laws. Parliament meets to pass laws in Harare, the country's capital. Zimbabwe's parliament is made up of two groups. As of 2023, the Senate has 80 members. The National Assembly has 270 members.

About 1.5 million people live in Zimbabwe's capital city of Harare.

The courts make up the judicial branch of Zimbabwe's government. They make rulings using the country's **constitution**. It lays out all of Zimbabwe's basic laws.

The president, two vice presidents, and the **cabinet** make up the executive branch of the government. The executive branch makes sure people follow the laws.

FACT!

Zimbabwe was the last African country to gain its independence from Britain.

GOVERNMENT CORRUPTION

Robert Mugabe became the leader of Zimbabwe in 1980. At first, people considered him to be a good leader. Later, people said he was guilty of **corruption**. Fellow leaders forced him to step down in 2017.

Emmerson Mnangagwa is Zimbabwe's president as of 2023.

THE ECONOMY

Zimbabwe is one of the 20 poorest countries in the world. This problem got worse in 2019 and 2020 for several reasons. In 2020, COVID-19 spread around the world. Many countries had economic problems because of this, including Zimbabwe.

FACT!

From 2007 to 2008, Zimbabwe had one of the worst cases of **hyperinflation** in history. At its worst point, prices doubled every day.

Sometimes kids have to work in Zimbabwe. These kids are hitting corn with sticks to make the **kernels** fall off the cob.

Another big problem for Zimbabwe is **climate change**. Most people in Zimbabwe are farmers. They grow crops such as tobacco, cotton, and sugar. As the planet heats up and the weather changes, crops sometimes fail. This costs farmers money.

A third problem for Zimbabwe is that its government doesn't always run the economy well. This makes it hard for people to earn enough money.

In the cities, many Zimbabweans have the same kinds of jobs as people in cities all over the world. This man is helping to build a house.

TRADING WITH OTHER COUNTRIES

Some of Zimbabwe's main trading partners are South Africa, China, Botswana, and the United States. It exports, or sells, tobacco, metals, and cotton. It imports, or buys, oil, food, and machines.

THE ENVIRONMENT

Zimbabwe has many of the animals people think of when they picture Africa. These include zebras, lions, elephants, rhinoceroses, and hippopotamuses. The country also has plants such as teak and mahogany— two trees that are highly prized for their wood.

Zimbabwe has problems with its environment, or natural world. Many of Zimbabwe's rivers and lakes are polluted, or dirty. This causes problems for people as well as animals. Also, people have cut down too many trees. This is called deforestation. They're clearing the land for farming and mining, but this takes homes away from animals.

FACT!
Clearing land for tobacco crops has been a major cause of deforestation in Zimbabwe in recent years.

TAKING CARE OF WILDLIFE

To keep animals safe from poachers, or illegal hunters, Zimbabwe has set up several national parks. The largest and best known is Hwange National Park. Tourists come every year to see the animals there.

A species, or kind, of pangolin known as Temminck's ground pangolin is the only species of pangolin **native** to Zimbabwe.

15

THE PEOPLE TODAY

Zimbabwe is home to several **ethnic groups**. Most of Zimbabwe's leaders belong to the largest group, called the Shona. Their homeland is called Mashonaland, and it makes up part of what is now northeastern Zimbabwe.

Traditional women's clothing in Zimbabwe includes a colorful wrap dress and matching head wrap.

SMALLER GROUPS

The Shona is one group that is made up of several smaller groups. These include the Manyika, Zezuru, Karanga, Korekore, and Ndau. Matabeleland is home to the Ndebele and the Kalanga—another ethnic group.

The second-largest group is the Ndebele. Many Ndebele people live in Matabeleland, the western third of the country. During much of Zimbabwe's history, the Shona and the Ndebele fought each other. Today, they get along much better. Each group has its own culture, or way of life.

Most Zimbabweans live in the countryside. Of those who live in the cities, most live in Harare and Bulawayo.

FACT!
About 16 million people live in Zimbabwe today.

Many Zimbabweans wear Western-style clothing.

LIFESTYLE

Life can be hard in Zimbabwe. About 62 percent of the people are poor. In the countryside, women and girls often do housework such as gathering firewood and water. Boys and men take care of the animals and crops.

FACT!

Many Zimbabweans have a virus called HIV. This can turn into a deadly disease called AIDS.

About 85 percent of boys and 86 percent of girls go to school in Zimbabwe.

In the city, women and men work in jobs outside the home. However, most people have trouble buying enough food and clothing for their families. Instead of paying for things with money, many people barter, or trade. Many people also have trouble paying for a doctor. This means they have to live with being sick. This makes living in crowded cities unsafe when people have diseases that are easy to spread.

GOVERNMENT CORRUPTION

In Harare, people pay the government money, or taxes. Taxes should be used for things such as fixing roads and buying new books for schools. During Mugabe's presidency, things were never fixed. This was a sign that government workers were taking that money for themselves.

Harare's streets are often full of litter.

RELIGION

Most Zimbabweans are Christian. However, the constitution says all Zimbabweans can follow any religion they want—or none at all. As much as 10 percent of the population has no religion.

This small building is a Christian church in Masvingo Province, Zimbabwe.

CONVERTING TO CHRISTIANITY

Missionaries are people who travel to other countries to try to get people to convert, or change, to a certain religion. Missionaries first brought Christianity to Zimbabwe in the mid-1500s.

Some Zimbabweans practice traditional Zimbabwean religions. Even people who are Christians still often practice parts of these religions. The Shona people believe in a god called Mwari. The Ndebele god is uMlimu. Zimbabweans who follow these religions believe they can talk to the gods through the spirits of their family members who have died. They believe people called spirit mediums can talk to the dead, and witches can talk to evil spirits.

FACT!
Some Zimbabweans are Jewish, Hindu, or Muslim.

These Zimbabwean children are reading the Christian Bible.

LANGUAGE

Shona is the most widely spoken language in Zimbabwe. Ndebele is the second most spoken language. Many people in Zimbabwe speak more than one language. English is also a common language. This is mainly because the British controlled the country for so long.

MANY OFFICIAL LANGUAGES

An official language is one the government uses. Zimbabwe's 16 official languages are Chewa, Chibarwe, English, Kalanga, Koisan, Nambya, Ndau, Ndebele, Shangani, Shona, Sign Language, Sotho, Tonga, Tswana, Venda, and Xhosa.

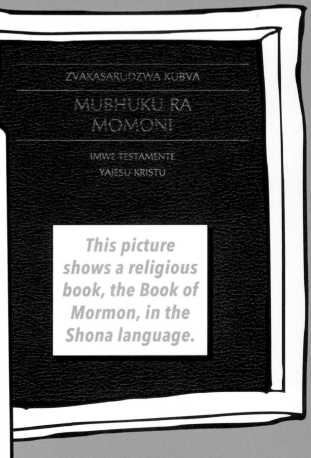

ZVAKASARUDZWA KUBVA

MUBHUKU RA MOMONI

IMWE TESTAMENTE YAJESU KRISTU

This picture shows a religious book, the Book of Mormon, in the Shona language.

Shona, Ndebele, and English are the languages most commonly used by the government, newspapers, radio, and TV. In the 20th century, many people started to complain about this. They said people weren't paying enough attention to the many other languages Zimbabweans speak. In response to this, the government changed the constitution in 2013 to give Zimbabwe 16 official languages.

FACT!
Even though English is widely spoken in Zimbabwe, most people learn it in school as a second language.

Many signs in Zimbabwe are written in English.

Daily Gazette
THREAT OF MORE STRIKES

DANGER
REPAIRING OF WATER MAINS

ARTS AND FESTIVALS

Art and music are important parts of Zimbabwean life. Traditional instruments include the *mbira* and the marimba. The mbira is very important to the Shona. People who follow traditional religions believe it can be used to talk with the spirits of dead family members. It's been played in Zimbabwe for thousands of years.

The British banned the mbira because they felt it wasn't a Christian instrument.

FACT!
There are cave paintings in Zimbabwe that are thousands of years old.

There are festivals throughout the year in Zimbabwe. Some are religious, like Easter. Others are connected to different ethnic groups. Zimbabwe also has several public holidays. Independence Day is on April 18. This holiday marks the day in 1980 when Zimbabwe became an independent nation.

VICTORIA FALLS CARNIVAL

Every year, people gather near Victoria Falls for the Vic Falls Carnival. This huge festival lets visitors see some of the best art and music Zimbabwe has to offer.

These Zimbabwean dolls are wearing traditional clothes made with cloth and beads.

FUN AND PLAY

Tourists often come to Zimbabwe to visit animal reserves, see Victoria Falls, and tour the remains of Great Zimbabwe. However, most people who live in Zimbabwe don't do those things every day.

TRADITIONAL GAMES

Zimbabweans play two games that are played all over the world. Kids play hide-and-seek. Adults and kids play a board game called tsoro. In other parts of the world, it's known as mancala, bao, ayo, and many other names.

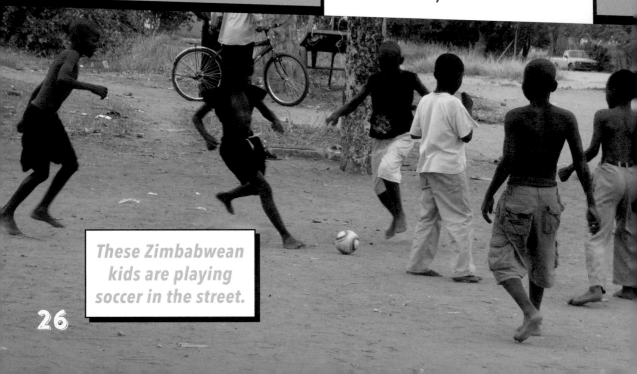

These Zimbabwean kids are playing soccer in the street.

Many Zimbabweans enjoy playing and watching sports. The most popular sport here is soccer, which Zimbabweans call football. Zimbabwe has national teams that play against teams from other countries. Cricket, which was brought to Zimbabwe by the British, is another popular sport. It is similar to baseball.

Zimbabweans also spend time playing games, singing, dancing, and making crafts. In the cities, many people watch TV and listen to music on the radio.

This picture shows an ancient tsoro board made from a piece of rock.

FACT!
As of 2023, Zimbabwe has won two Olympic gold medals in swimming and one in field hockey.

FOOD

Corn is served in some form at almost every meal in Zimbabwe. *Sadza* is a cornmeal porridge, or type of cereal. It can be sweetened for breakfast and served unsweetened with vegetables at lunch. The leftovers are used to make a drink called *munya*. Sadza is also served alongside other dishes, such as *muboora*, which is a soup made with pumpkin leaves.

Shown here is gango, or ngago ("frying pan" in Shona), served with sadza. Gango is a dish made with meat and vegetables.

Zimbabweans don't eat meat such as beef or chicken often because many people can't afford it. However, a small fish called kapenta can be found in Lake Tanganyika and the Zambezi River. People who live near these bodies of water often eat the fish as a snack.

BUGS FOR BREAKFAST

Zimbabweans who live in the countryside often eat bugs with their meals. Mopane worms, crickets, and flying ants are some examples. They are healthy and keep people full.

FACT!

Peanuts and fruit are common in many Zimbabwean dishes.

Shown here is the fruit of a baobab, a type of tree that grows in Zimbabwe.

GLOSSARY

cabinet: A group of advisers who help the political head of a government.

climate change: Changes in the Earth's weather over time due to human actions.

constitution: A document that lays out the laws of a country.

corruption: Dishonest behavior by those in power.

economic: Relating to the way goods and services are made and sold.

ethnic group: A group of people who share the same culture and often the same language.

hyperinflation: When money loses its value very quickly over a short period of time.

kernel: A whole grain or seed of a cereal, such as wheat or corn.

native: Belonging to a particular area.

plateau: A flat area of high ground.

republic: A type of government in which people vote for their leaders.

traditional: Having to do with the ways of doing things in a culture that are passed down from parents to children.

FIND OUT MORE

Books

Atinuke. *Africa, Amazing Africa*. Somerville, MA: Candlewick Press, 2021.

Laroche, Giles. *Lost Cities*. Boston, MA: Houghton Mifflin Harcourt, 2019.

Spanier, Kristine. *Zimbabwe*. Minneapolis, MN: Jump!, 2020.

Websites

Ducksters: Zimbabwe
www.ducksters.com/geography/country.php?country=Zimbabwe
Read more interesting facts about Zimbabwe.

Kiddle: Zimbabwe
kids.kiddle.co/Zimbabwe
Learn all about Zimbabwe.

Video

YouTube: "Victoria Falls—Zimbabwe"
www.youtube.com/watch?v=H0LG5rOo_9w
Take a look at some beautiful views of Victoria Falls.

INDEX

A
agriculture, 4, 7, 13–14, 18
arts, 4, 24–25, 27

B
Britain, 9, 11, 22, 24

C
clothing, 16–17, 19, 25
COVID-19, 12

E
economy, 8–9, 12–13, 18–19
education, 18, 23

F
food, 5, 12–13, 19, 28–29

G
government, 9–11, 13, 19–20, 23
Great Zimbabwe, 5, 8, 26

H
Harare, 10, 17, 19
health, 18–19
history, 8–9, 11

I
independence, 9, 25

L
lakes, 4, 14, 29

M
Mnangagwa, Emmerson, 11
Mugabe, Robert, 9, 11, 19

N
Ndebele people/language, 16–17, 21–23

R
religion, 8, 20–21, 24–25
rivers, 6, 14, 29

S
Shona people/language, 8, 16–17, 21–24
sports, 4, 26–27

V
Victoria Falls, 6, 26

W
wildlife, 4–5, 14–15, 26